Taking Godly Care of the Earth

Stewardship Lessons in Creation Care

by Anna Layton Sharp

Illustrated by Russ Flint

Carson-Dellosa Christian Publishing
Greensboro, North Carolina

It is the mission of Carson-Dellosa Christian Publishing to create the highest-quality Scripture-based children's products that teach the Word of God, share His love and goodness, assist in faith development, and glorify His Son, Jesus Christ.

". . . teach me your ways so I may know you. . . ."
Exodus 33:13

For Dad,
You must have taken me on one too many nature hikes;
this book will reveal that you accidentally raised a liberal tree-hugger.
Thank you for introducing me to the wonder of creation
—in the forest, through a telescope, and under rocks.

Credits
Author: Anna Layton Sharp
Editor: Carol Layton
Illustrator: Russ Flint
Cover Design: Annette Hollister-Papp
Cover Illustration: Russ Flint
Layout Design: Mark Conrad
© 2000 PhotoDisc. Inc.

Introduction

Christian schools have wonderful opportunity—and responsibility—to teach environmental stewardship. As creation is being polluted and destroyed at unprecedented rates, "tending the garden" is not only an act of worship—protecting the Earth's water, air, and soil is an essential part of loving our neighbor. This book can get you started on your way to a creation-minded classroom.

Table of Contents

Teacher tips, calendar, and resources.. page 4
>Ideas to create an eco-friendly classroom and lead by Christian example.

Chapter 1—Our first responsibility .... page 9
>Taking a closer look at dominion and our responsibility to God's creation, this chapter helps students care for the earth through lessons in reducing, reusing, and recycling.

Chapter 2—The rainbow covenant .... page 19
>This chapter contains a variety of rainbow-themed activities to teach students about God's covenant with every living creature.

Chapter 3—Whose Earth is it, anyway? .... page 30
>If we're only strangers and guests, we better wipe our feet! In this chapter, students learn more ways to faithfully take care of God's Earth.

Chapter 4—The other evangelist .... page 44
>This chapter helps students think about creation as a worldwide witness to the glory of God—and learn how they can support this unique "missionary."

Chapter 5—Outdoor learning .... page 54
>In this chapter, teachers and students learn more about God's custom-made classroom, and how they can develop their own natural learning playground.

Chapter 6—Our neighbors in the rainforest .... page 63
>This chapter helps students understand how caring for the rainforest is a way to show our love for God and our neighbor.

Scripture index .... page 77
Answer key.. page 80

Teacher Tips

For a Creation-Minded Classroom

We know that kids may take or leave what we say, but they naturally tend to do as we do. "Set an example for the believers" (I Timothy 4:12) by sharing your organic garden's first strawberries, talking to students about your volunteer work at the food pantry, even arriving to school winded from your bike ride!

Traffic may prevent younger students from walking or biking to school, but adults within reasonable distance have no excuse. Offer to accompany students who live in your neighborhood.

We have a wonderful world on loan from God. To learn about it and Him, there's no substitute for hands-on experience. Take students outdoors as much as possible. Does your school yard have a meadow or forest? Does a stream run through the property? Take advantage of the learning opportunities these ecosystems offer. Or jump right in, plant a garden, and start breaking new ground—literally!

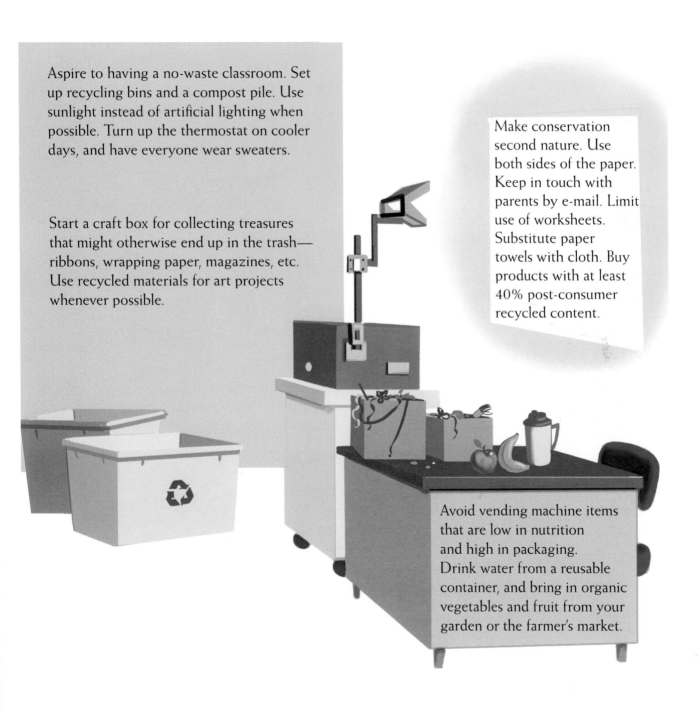

Aspire to having a no-waste classroom. Set up recycling bins and a compost pile. Use sunlight instead of artificial lighting when possible. Turn up the thermostat on cooler days, and have everyone wear sweaters.

Start a craft box for collecting treasures that might otherwise end up in the trash—ribbons, wrapping paper, magazines, etc. Use recycled materials for art projects whenever possible.

Make conservation second nature. Use both sides of the paper. Keep in touch with parents by e-mail. Limit use of worksheets. Substitute paper towels with cloth. Buy products with at least 40% post-consumer recycled content.

Avoid vending machine items that are low in nutrition and high in packaging. Drink water from a reusable container, and bring in organic vegetables and fruit from your garden or the farmer's market.

A Year of Creation Care

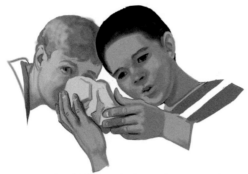

On **January** 7th, Old Rock Day, have students bring in fossils and other interesting minerals for show-and-tell.

During National Bird Feeding Month in **February**, learn how to create a bird-friendly school yard.

Follow-up Earth Day festivities in **April** by relaxing in the shade of your favorite tree on Arbor Day.

Celebrate **May** Day with outdoor games and lots of "a-maying." Have students collect wildflower garlands to share with nursing home residents.

March is a great time to plan a garden. Schedule planting day for the first day of spring, or spring equinox. Explain to students that day and night are the same length during an equinox. Remind them of Genesis 1:4, when God divides night and day.

Enjoy **June** 21, the 1st day of summer, or summer solstice, by snacking on the last of your garden's strawberries or the very first peaches.

Starting with Build a Scarecrow Day (July 1st), and ending with Salad Week, **July** is the gardener's month.

Help students organize a school-wide paper recycling drive. The third week in **October** is National Forest Products Week.

Encourage students to try walking, biking, or carpooling the first week of school—**August** is Clean Air Month.

Remind students to be thankful for God's bountiful creation—just like the pilgrims did at the first Thanksgiving. Remember the Native Americans who shared their harvest, and study their creation-minded beliefs during **November**—Native American Heritage Month.

Encourage students to prepare for a Christmas that celebrates Jesus, not Madison Avenue. Charity drives in **December** offer many opportunities for students to donate their favorite toys to a shelter, or have students think of homemade or Earth-friendly gifts to exchange.

The new fall colors of the autumnal equinox in **September** provide the perfect opportunity for learning about photosynthesis.

Organizations and resources

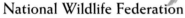

National Wildlife Federation
Backyard Wildlife Habitat
11100 Wildlife Center Drive
Reston, VA 20190-5362
800-822-9919
www.nwf.org
info@nwf.org

Green Teacher
P.O. Box 452
Niagara Falls, NY 14304-0452
(416) 960-1244
www.greenteacher.org
info@greenteacher.com

Environmental Protection Agency
Ariel Rios Building
1200 Pennsylvania Avenue, N.W.
Washington, DC 20460
(202) 272-0167
www.epa.gov/teachers
public-access@epa.gov

Evangelical Environmental Network
10 East Lancaster Avenue
Wynnewood, PA 19096
(610) 645-9390
www.esa-online.org
een@esa-online.org

National Religious Partnership for the Environment
49 South Pleasant Street, Suite 301
Amherst, MA 01002
(413) 253-1515
www.nrpe.org
nrpe@nrpe.org

Target Earth
(formerly the Christian
Environmental Association)
3015-P Hopyard Road
Pleasanton, CA 94588
(925) 462-2439
www.targetearth.org
info@targetearth.org

Recommended reading

Earth-Wise: A Biblical Response to Environmental Issues by Calvin B. DeWitt. CRC Publications, 1994. An excellent stewardship primer by a passionate environmental studies professor and Christian. Formatted for use by study groups.

Loving Nature: Ecological Integrity and Christian Responsibility by James A. Nash. Abingdon Press, 1991. Covers a broad range of concerns in a balanced and thoughtful manner.

The Comforting Whirlwind: God, Job, and the Scale of Creation by Bill McKibben. Eerdmans, 1994. A reflection on consumer culture and Christian values.

Beyond Ecophobia: Reclaiming the Heart in Nature Education by David Sobel. Orion Society, 1996. Speaks to teachers, parents, or others interested in nurturing in children the ability to understand and care for nature.

Chapter 1— Our first responsibility

God spoke: "Let us make human beings in our image, make them reflecting our nature so they can be responsible for the fish in the sea, the birds in the air, the cattle, and, yes, Earth itself, and every animal that moves on the face of Earth."
Genesis 1:26 THE MESSAGE

The Message version of Genesis 1:26 sheds light on an often misunderstood verse. In many translations, God instructs man to "have dominion over" animals. Some people have misinterpreted the word dominion and used this passage to justify exploiting animals and their habitats for selfish reasons. Having dominion is the opposite of neglect or misuse—it means that God has entrusted us with the care of His creation.

Did you know?

Jesus serves as our example of dominion. ~~Have students look up Philippians 2:7~~: "[He] made himself nothing, taking the very nature of a servant." *Phil 2:7*

Stewardship to the Earth is not God's afterthought. ~~Have students look up~~ Genesis 2:15. What is one of the very first things God has Adam do? What are some ways we can tend the garden today?

God declared creation "good" many times before man ever arrived on the scene! (Genesis 1) God created plants and animals to live in perfect harmony—what we call a balanced ecosystem. How can people upset this harmony? How can they be part of it?

Selected Literature

Animals Nobody Loves by Seymour Simon: SeaStar Books, 2001. Tells us why even the ickiest creatures should be appreciated. Use this book to remind students that God loves the animals that nobody else does!

Animals of the Bible by Mary Hoffman: Phyllis Fogelman Books, 2003. Nine Old Testament stories are illustrated to depict all of the animals, even insects, with dignity and beauty.

Genesis by Ed Young: HarperCollins Children's Books, 1997. Stunning abstract illustrations slowly take form to tell the story of Creation.

What a big responsibility!

Have students think of ways people use their authority in good ways. For example, a parent caring for a child and Jesus' love for us. Tell students that "having dominion" over the earth is not an excuse to use it any way we want. Instead, it is a great responsibility that we should not abuse. How can we care for the earth as our parents care for us?

Picture the Solution

Take photographs of your own community—a polluted river, an expanded highway, a forest being destroyed to make way for a new neighborhood or shopping mall. If possible, allow students to take their own pictures. Have them discuss the problems they see in the photographs and think of solutions. For example, car-riders could take the bus instead—reducing highway traffic and the need for a highway expansion. Post these solutions on an award chart, and mark students' progress in meeting different goals.

Look closely

One of the greatest impacts people have on animals is how we treat their habitats. Explain to students that while they would not tear down a bird's nest or hurt animals intentionally, other things we do can damage God's creation. Reproduce, or share with students, the illustration on page 11. Tell students to find and circle examples of people mistreating the Earth.

At first, students may not see problems because the scene is a typical afternoon for many families. Encourage the students to look closer. See the child's granola bar? An apple would be a better snack choice—there's no leftover trash. Notice the empty backseats? Why not give some friends a ride home from school? Fewer cars on the road mean less gasoline and less pollution. Even the school yard could be improved—instead of lawn there could be a garden, woodland, or meadow. Unlike lawn, natural areas require no mowing, pesticide, or herbicide.

Name _____

Look Closely

Look closely at the picture. Find and circle examples of people mistreating the Earth. On the back of the page, explain Earth-friendly changes that could be made.

What a waste!

Materials

paper and plastic grocery bags

weighing scale

Help students understand how much garbage they generate. Set aside "responsibility days" to measure how much trash the class produces. Instead of using the school's trash cans, have students keep all waste—from leftover lunch to paper towels—in grocery bags brought from home. Use separate bags for items that can be composted (food) or recycled (paper, glass, plastic, aluminum). (See page 15 for composting instructions.)

Each day for a week, weigh a student volunteer first with and then without the bags. Record the weights of the materials on the reproducible chart on page 13. Repeat this activity every few weeks. Mark improvements on the class calendar. Encourage students to try this experiment at home.

This activity provides lots of opportunities for students to hone math skills. They can figure out how many pounds of trash the class would generate in a week, month, or year. Have students calculate how much waste they can save from the landfill (recyclable and compost items).

WE'RE MAKING A DiFFERENCE!

1.5 pounds of paper Per Day

270 pounds of paper PER School Year!

Mrs. Minwalla's Class Saved:

22 pounds of paper

3 pounds aluminum cans

8 pounds of glass

from the landfill this month!

We recycled 17% more in February than we did in January!

Use the collected waste to teach students about recycling. Divide recyclables into glass, plastic, paper, and aluminum. Does your school have recycling bins? If not, check if the county or city offers a pick-up service. Students can team with other classes to create and share hallway recycling bins.

"Let nothing be wasted." John 6:12
—Jesus

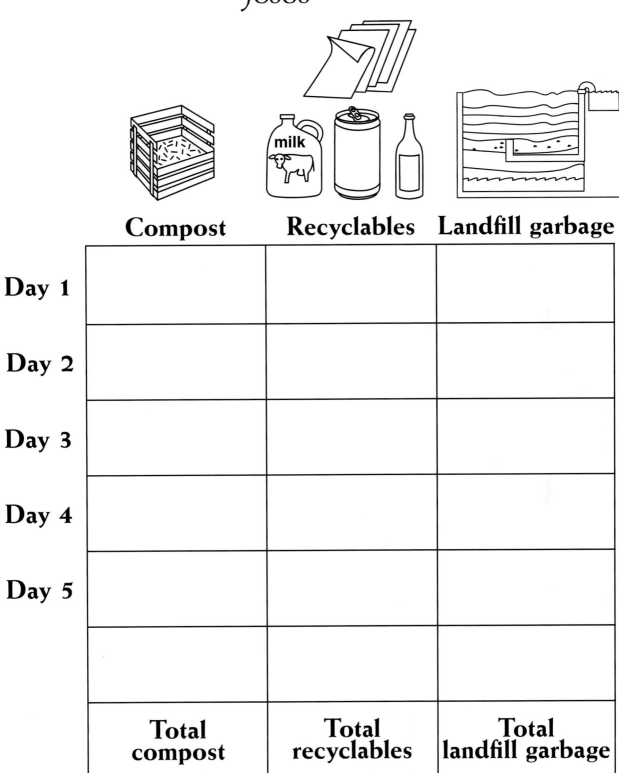

	Compost	Recyclables	Landfill garbage
Day 1			
Day 2			
Day 3			
Day 4			
Day 5			
	Total compost	**Total recyclables**	**Total landfill garbage**

Trash can warnings

Keep students thinking about waste by coloring and posting reminders over trash cans. Provide students with copies of the Scripture index on pages 77-79. They can use the verses as inspiration to create their own reminders.

Make the most of it—compost it

Put the students' collected banana peels and bread crusts to good use by creating a classroom compost bin. Composting biodegradable items turns them into a rich soil that fertilizes plants—and saves them from the landfill.

To compost outdoors, alternate layers of soil, food scraps, leaves, and grass clippings and keep moist. Cover with a tarp in rainy weather. Mix the pile every week to aerate and circulate the materials to different areas of the pile. *Don't use any meat in your compost* (including waste from dogs, cats, and other carnivores), bones or grease, and dairy products. The occasional eggshell is okay.

A mini-composting station can be made in a clear plastic container. Add soil to the bottom of the container, and then layer yard clippings and food waste. Continue layering, sprinkling water between layers (do not soak). Cover with plastic wrap, prick with a pin, and let the mixture set for several weeks. Stir the compost each week and keep moist. Let students observe the materials decomposing. Because the decomposing materials may have a noticeable odor, you may want to keep the station in a covered place outdoors.

Use the compost for a class planting project, or donate to a neighbor's garden.

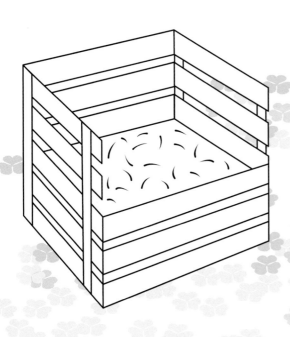 

Even better than recycling

Be sure to mention to students that the recycling process still uses energy and creates waste. The best way to conserve is to reduce consumption—for example, drinking water from the tap instead of buying a can of soda. Have each student think of at least one way he can avoid creating trash that day at school. Use these suggestions as starting points:

USE CLOTH TOWEL OR AIR DRY HANDS AFTER WASHING

CHOOSE FRUITS OR VEGETABLES OVER PRE-PACKAGED SNACKS

USE BOTH SIDES OF PAPER FOR WRITING

USE WASHABLE INSTEAD OF DISPOSABLE CUTLERY

GO WITHOUT A DRINKING STRAW

USE PENCILS AFTER THE ERASER IS GONE

Obey God—not your thirst. So you gave up your soda for a glass of water—does it really make a difference? Some environmental problems may seem overwhelming, but remind students that God tells us "nothing will be impossible for you." Matthew 17:20. Discuss how one person really can change the world.

The Bible is chock full of individuals who chose to obey God instead of doing their own thing. Even though it was hard, they did as God told them and it made a huge difference! Just think of Moses, David, Esther—even the boy who provided Jesus with bread and fish to feed the crowd! Have students think of other examples.

Landfill

Explain to students that when we throw garbage "away," it really just goes somewhere else. We bury most of our garbage in landfills. If there is a landfill near you, plan a class trip. Landfills are impressive to see first-hand. Before your visit, explain how landfills are created.

First, the ground is lined with a protective layer of clay or plastic to keep waste from seeping into the ground. Some waste still leaks out, but builders try not to let it get into the groundwater. Decomposing trash creates landfill gas, which is made up mostly of methane and carbon dioxide. A system of pipes is built into the landfill to collect and release the gas. This gas contributes to smog and global warming, but people are finding ways to use it as an energy source. What does your local landfill do with the gas?

A day's worth of garbage is compacted into a "cell" and covered with dirt. Because there is no air inside, the garbage can't break down. In a landfill, a plastic cup and a banana peel could both last thousands of years without decomposing! Groups of cells eventually make up a whole mountain of garbage that is covered with another liner and more dirt. The landfill is then covered with grass and other plants. Instead of heaps of garbage, you see what appears to be green rolling hills!

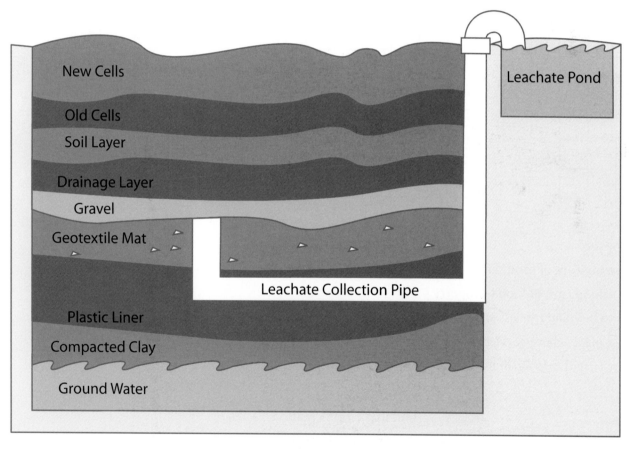

Remind students of Matthew 23:28: ". . . on the outside you appear to people as righteous but on the inside you are full of hypocrisy and wickedness." How does a landfill reveal our own hypocrisy? Have students look up the word hypocrisy and share the definition with the class. Do some people pretend to love God and His creation and then treat it badly? Use the landfill to illustrate this point: it looks natural and grassy on the outside but it is really full of garbage. Encourage students to continue thinking of ways they can truly be good to the Earth—inside and out.

Creation Crossword

ACROSS

1. a mixture of food scraps, grass, and leaves that breaks down, becoming rich soil

5. taking care of God's property

9. to buy and use less stuff

10. a place where garbage is stored

11. to use things again instead of throwing them away

DOWN

1. protecting God's creation

2. chemical used to kill pests, especially insects

3. a plant or animal's house

4. when people hide their sin and pretend to be good

6. power to influence and make decisions, responsibility

7. chemical used to kill plants, especially weeds

8. to put something through a special process so that it can be used again

Chapter 2—The rainbow covenant

"Whenever the rainbow appears in the clouds, I will see it and remember the everlasting covenant between God and all living creatures of every kind on the earth." Genesis 9:16

Most people know about Noah and the rainbow—but some Christian educators overlook one of the most interesting things about this covenant: it is between God and every last living creature on Earth. Have students read Genesis 9:12-17 and count the number of times the phrase "every living creature" is repeated. God made sure to emphasize over and over His love for *all* of creation—not just mankind. The rainbow is a beautiful reminder that God cares for each and every creature. Because God made us to reflect His nature, we should also appreciate and care for every living creature on Earth.

Did you know?

Two people never see the same rainbow. The colors of the rainbow are distributed in a unique way to each observer's eye. Each of your two eyes even sees its own rainbow. Doesn't God give us the most unique gifts!

There are rainbow colors, such as ultraviolet, that the human eye can't see—but some birds and bees can. Not only did God make the rainbow covenant with all creatures, He made parts of the rainbow especially for them!

After it rains, the air smells fresh and clean because the water cleans the air when it falls and takes the pollution right out of the sky. Unfortunately, the pollution then contaminates the land.

Selected Literature

A Prayer for the Earth: The Story of Naamah, Noah's Wife by Sandy Eisenberg Sasso: Jewish Lights Publishing, 1996. Noah's wife collects seeds to keep on the ark to later replant the earth.

All the Colors of the Rainbow by Alan Fowler: Children's Press, 1999. Fun and informative book that answers many rainbow hows and whys.

Rainbows are Made: Poems by Carl Sandburg by Lee Hopkins: Harcourt, 1984. Beautiful wood engravings accompany delightful Sandburg poems.

Rainbow safari

Every time it rains you have an opportunity to spot a rainbow. Rainbows aren't just pretty surprises—they're powerful signs from God. It would be a shame to miss one! Make it a regular class activity. After every rain shower, spend a few minutes on a rainbow hunt.

Hint #1 Your chances for observing a rainbow are much better in warmer weather. Explain to students that rainbows form as light passes through water. Why do you rarely see rainbows when it's cold? Because frozen water droplets cannot reflect sunlight.

Hint #2 The sun is always behind you when you face a rainbow. To see a rainbow, you need to be between the sun and the rain.

What does a rainbow look like through dark glasses?
If you look at a rainbow with polarized sunglasses, part of the rainbow will disappear! When light is reflected at certain angles it becomes polarized. A rainbow's angle of reflection is close to the angle of reflection at which sunlight is polarized.

Save the worms!

After it rains, do you notice worms stranded on the sidewalk? Talk to the students about ways that people disrupt the habitats of animals. Students may mention current topics such as drilling in Alaska or destruction of rainforests. Remind them of local concerns, too, such as the construction of a new mall. Each student can research an example of humans damaging animals' habitats. The Environmental Protection Agency web site (www.epa.gov) allows you to search for environmental issues by zip code. You can also use the following topics as starting points:

Pesticides and herbicides used in gardens and lawns kill harmful critters as well as beneficial animals such as ladybugs, worms, spiders, and honeybees.

Very few trees are salvaged when new housing developments are planned.

New stores, churches, restaurants, theaters, and other buildings are often constructed even though there are already vacant buildings available.

Don't forget to rescue the marooned worm!

Rainbow party

When a rainbow is spotted, celebrate with these activities:

Guest list

Who's invited to your rainbow party? What sorts of animals come out to play after a rainstorm? Do you see birds feeding on insects in the grass? Burrowing insects and other creatures come up to the surface to escape excess moisture. Mark off an area outside and have students get a rough count of insects, worms, and other critters that are visible on the ground's surface. Compare these results with findings on a dry day.

Eat a rainbow

We think of rainbows as having seven colors: red, orange, yellow, green, blue, indigo, and violet—but rainbows also contain all the colors in between. Keep handy a healthy and colorful snack: a Rainbow Trail Mix of dried cranberries, banana chips, green pumpkin seeds, blue corn tortilla chips, dried plums, and raisins, and serve with orange juice. You have a treat worthy of Roy G. Biv himself—but remind students that God puts more colors in a real rainbow than we can even imagine!

Color the rainbow

Provide crayons and paper for students to sketch the rainbow. Compare these drawings to ones done earlier from imagination. Discuss how the drawings differ. What new observations have the students made?

Indoor rainbows

Students may also create rainbows of their own. Although "artificial" rainbows don't match the grandeur of natural ones, they're easy and fun. Make rainbows using the following techniques, and have students record each with drawings. Discuss how the rainbows are similar and different.

Place a clear shallow glass or plastic pan in sunlight. Fill the container with water. Rest a mirror on the bottom of the pan, with its top edge leaning out of the water. Light will bend and separate into colors as it enters the water. As the light leaves the water, it will bend again and further separate the colors.

Spray water mist from a hose. Sunlight shining through the water droplets should create a color spectrum.

View a water droplet on a leaf close-up—an inch from your eye. At a certain angle you may catch a nice bit of color!

Hold a prism between the light source and a plain surface such as a ceiling, wall, or white paper.

 CD-204010 *Taking Godly Care of the Earth*

What makes you see red?
(and orange, and yellow, and green . . .)

Use the students' rainbow drawings to discuss how the eye perceives color. Although the sun's rays appear colorless, the rays contain all the colors of the rainbow mixed together. This mixture is known as white light. Each of the colors in white light bends at a slightly different angle because it has a different wave length. Red has the longest wave length and violet the shortest. All other rainbow colors fall in between, in a definite order—red, orange, yellow, green, blue, indigo, and violet.

When white light strikes a white crayon, it appears white because the crayon absorbs no color and reflects all colors equally. A black crayon absorbs all colors equally and reflects none, so it looks black. Artists consider black a color, but scientists do not, because black is the absence of all color. Have students describe which colors are absorbed or reflected off their rainbow drawings. For example, if a crayon mark looks green, the mark actually contains no green. All the green is bounced off, so the mark only appears to be green.

Rainbow maxims

(See page 24 worksheet.) Discuss the sayings on page 24 that describe the connection between weather and rainbows. What do they have in common? Do they seem reliable? For example, "Rainbow in the morning gives you fair warning" makes sense because the sun is in the east in the morning, and the shower and associated rainbow are in the west. Since weather generally moves from west to east, rain is approaching. What can we make of "Rainbow to windward, foul fall the day; rainbow to leeward, damp runs away?" If wind is coming from the direction of the rainbow, the rain is heading toward you. If the rainbow is in the opposite direction, the rain has passed you.

Cast your net: rainbow trout and other fish

(See page 25 worksheet.) The rainbow trout is a very popular North American game fish. Rainbow trout and other fish are sometimes taken out of their natural habitats and introduced to foreign areas for fishing. Scientists say that introduced fish, known as aliens, never have a good impact on the environment. Jesus often used fish to teach a lesson. Remind students of the importance of fish in the Gospels as they complete the worksheet.

Name _____

Read the maxims and explain their meanings.

Rainbow Maxims

1. Rainbow at night, shepherd's delight;
rainbow in morning, shepherds take warning.

_____

_____

2. Rainbow to windward, foul fall the day;
rainbow to leeward, damp runs away.

_____

_____

3. Rainbow afternoon, good weather coming soon.

_____

_____

4. Rainbow in the morning
gives you fair warning.

_____

_____

_____

_____

_____

BONUS
What saying did Jesus tell us that
fishermen used to forecast weather?
(See Matthew 16:2-3.)

_____

_____

Name _____

Jesus Teaches with Fish

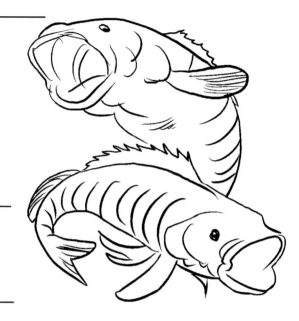

Look up the verses to answer the questions.

1. What did Jesus feed the multitude? (John 6:1-14)

    _____

2. What does Jesus tell His followers to do with the
    leftover food? (John 6:12)

    _____

3. Why would Jesus warn against wasting food even though he provided plenty? What does this tell us
    about how we should treat other resources God has given us?

    _____

4. To what can we compare God's kingdom? (Matthew 13:47)

    _____

5. Where does Jesus tell Peter to find the money to pay their taxes? (Matthew 17:24-27)

    _____

6. What did Simon, Andrew, and James do for a
    living before they met Jesus? (Mark 1:16)

    _____

    _____

7. What miracle caused these fishermen to leave
    their boats and follow Jesus? (Luke 5:1-11)

    _____

    _____

    _____

Cast your net

Have each student research a food fish. The Audubon Society, Monterey Bay Aquarium, and National Resources Defense Council all provide information about whether or not certain fish are farmed and harvested responsibly. Sometimes a fishery hurts other creatures (such as dolphins) or is poorly regulated. Other fish are bad to eat because they are endangered or tend to contain mercury. Students may use the following lists as a starting point for their own research.

Good
Wild Alaskan salmon
Farmed freshwater catfish
Mahi mahi
Pacific halibut
Squid

Bad
Atlantic and Pacific salmon
Shrimp
Wild oysters
Scallops

Tip: *Enhance this lesson with a field trip to a local fishery.*

For advanced classes Have students use the worksheet on page 27 to organize their findings before sharing and discussing what they've learned. For example, is there a relationship between how a fish is harvested and its price? Was a certain grocery store more knowledgeable and helpful in answering students' questions? With what they've learned, are students going to avoid eating certain fish? Did they discover other fish they want to try?

Name _____

Fish Files

Name of fish:_____   Circle one: freshwater or saltwater

Where this fish lives in the wild:_____

Where this fish is farmed: _____

Is this fish harvested responsibly? _____

Is it popular for sport fishing? _____

Is it native to its environment or is it an alien fish?_____

How is this fish harvested? (dragging, dredging, harpoon, etc.) _____

Does harvesting this fish hurt other animals? _____

Is this fish population over-fished or endangered? _____

Could this fish contain unsafe levels of mercury? _____

If your fish is sold at the grocery store:

    Name of grocery store: _____

    Cost of fish: $_____ per pound

Ask the butcher about your fish. How much information does he have? _____

_____

Is it the same or different from the information you collected in your own research?

_____

Rainbow cactus

Another rainbow namesake is the rainbow cactus which is native to the southwestern United Sates and Mexico. Its spines completely cover the stem, providing protection from intense sun. At different times of the year, the spines grow in bands of different colors. After a few years, the cactus' spines create a rainbow! As a reminder of God's covenant with every living creature, have each student create her own rainbow cactus out of recycled materials.

Materials

Cardboard or other stiff paper
Paper in different colors
Large cardboard tubes
Glue

Directions

For both the stiff and colored papers, have students recycle junk mail postcards, empty tissue boxes, old manila folders, and magazines. Cut stiff paper into rainbow cactus shape. Have students cover cacti with rainbow-colored "spines" made from short strips of the colored paper. To make the cactus stand-up, adhere to the cardboard tube.

Name _____

Every Living Creature Word Safari

Whenever the rainbow appears in the clouds, I will see it and remember the everlasting covenant between God and all living creatures of every kind on the earth. Genesis 9:16

```
S Y H Y E O V O A E M R T C R
F L C O V E N A N T R Z F W O
S Q Y N V A C Y R Z B W B D B
M H N P B E N E F I C I A L S
M A J V X D G U U T N F I Q C
S R L E Z S X H Q H R G H O M
K V U T A X R Z Y P W S F R P
E E R A I N B O W M I G A E Z
D S H J O K G C I F A F G Z N
M T J G X R Q J N N H X E Q Y
C U E O B F J E V S Y J I Z K
E X S A W O I W I B P Y Q M T
N I G J S L G F Q W B K D A Q
V P H C A O J M X T X H Q W D
N J Y T Y J R Y B S N S O B L
```

Find these words in the puzzle above. Words can be found across, down, and diagonally.

Word Bank

covenant	a promise
rainbow	an arc of colors formed by light passing through raindrops or mist
beneficials	critters that are good for gardens
maxim	a saying that comes from experience or observation
alien fish	fish that are moved into a foreign habitat by people
fish farm	tanks or ponds where fish are raised to sell for food
harvest	to gather food

         CD-204010 *Taking Godly Care of the Earth*

Chapter 3—Who's Earth is it, anyway?

The earth is the LORD's, and everything in it. Psalm 24:1

Psalm 24:1 is key to understanding our role as Earth stewards. The oceans, forests, and animals belong to God—even the trees and birds in our backyards. We are only caretakers, and one day we'll give the Master back His property. We all want to hear these joyful words: "Well done, good and faithful servant!" (Matthew 25:21)

As children, we may have learned that American Indians traded their land to European settlers for worthless trinkets—and we wondered at their foolishness. But selling or buying land was a foreign custom to most Native Americans. They knew that creation could only belong to God. At first, they may have traded with Europeans out of courtesy, and later out of fear. Whose beliefs were more in line with God's law—the Christians settlers or the "pagan" Indians?

Did you know?

If we're only guests, we should wipe our feet! Have students look up Leviticus 25:23. What does it mean that we are only strangers, guests, tenants, or aliens on the land? Talk with students about how guests are supposed to behave.

Selected Literature

People of the Breaking Day by Marcia Sewell: Atheneum, 1990. Learn how Wampanoag Indians lived with the natural world before European settlers arrived.

I Have Enough Stuff by Connie Beyer Horn: Concordia Publishing House, 1998. Toys, pets, clothes . . . what can students call their own, and what belongs to God?

Picture it

In Leviticus chapters 25 and 26, God gives specific directions for taking care of His property, the Earth. God says that the land must observe a Sabbath. Read what God says will happen if we don't allow the land to rest. We can see these consequences today—share the following illustrations with students. Do they look like wastelands and deserts?

Tropical deforestation scars the land and causes mosquito and rat populations to increase.

The absence of hedgerows causes erosion in crop fields and in housing developments.

Farmland becomes unproductive when crops are grown continuously for many seasons. Pesticides, herbicides, and fertilizers pollute water. The overgrazing of cattle causes the land to become dry and barren.

Have students look up Isaiah 5:8 to find out what God has to say about hedgerows and urban sprawl! Then, brainstorm ways that students can contribute to a solution to wastelands.

- eat less beef (or none), find and support a local farm that grazes their herds responsibly
- shop for produce at local farmers' markets
- grow fruits and vegetables in a neighborhood, school, church, or home garden
- eat fruits and vegetables that are in season
- urge local restaurants and grocers to buy locally-grown produce

Stewardship

Ask students to name examples of stewards—people who take care of other people's property. For example, gardeners tend your school yard, bankers invest your parents' money, dry cleaners press your dad's shirts, and mechanics fix your mom's car. What if mom picked her car up at the mechanic and it was still broken? What if the mechanic said, "Sorry, ma'am, the car is exactly like you left it." He wouldn't be a mechanic for very long!

Read Matthew 25:14-30 together. Jesus makes it clear that stewards can't just sit back and wait for their masters to return—they have to work hard taking care of the master's property.

Earth-friendly cleaners

Keeping tidy is sometimes dirty work—regular cleaning products can contain dangerous chemicals. Bring window cleaner and furniture polish to class, and have students read the ingredients and warning labels. Explain how these chemicals can end up in the water, soil—even in our bodies. Homemade cleaners don't contain dangerous chemicals, and there is less packaging and waste. Copy the Earth-friendly cleaning recipes on pages 33-34 for students to take home to share with their families. Have students try at least one recipe over the weekend, and report the results.

All-Purpose Cleaner

4 tablespoons baking soda
4 cups warm water

Dissolve baking soda in warm water. Place in a spray bottle or use from a wash pan. Apply with a sponge. Rinse with clear water.

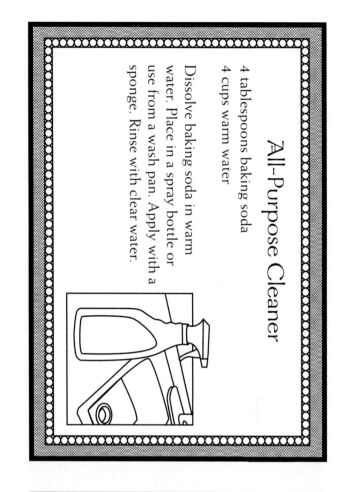

Window Cleaner

1 tablespoon white vinegar
1 cup water

Combine ingredients in a spray bottle. Spray on glass or mirrors and wipe with a clean cloth.

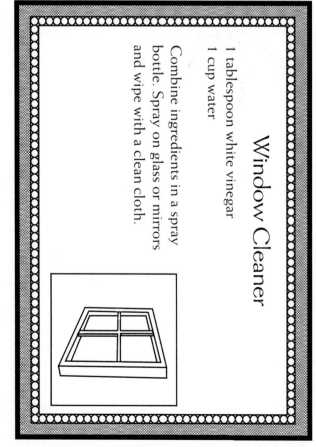

Drain Cleaner

½ cup baking soda
1 cup white vinegar

Pour baking soda down drain and follow with vinegar. Cover drain until fizzing stops. Flush drain with boiling water (an adult's job).

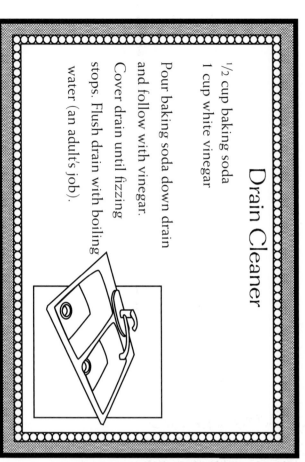

Furniture Polish

½ cup olive oil
¼ cup lemon juice

Mix together until well blended. Use a clean, soft cloth to apply to furniture.

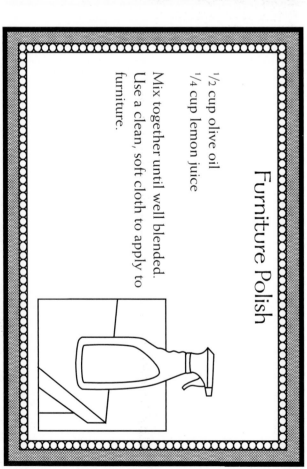

CD-204010 *Taking Godly Care of the Earth*

All-Purpose Cleaner

On a scale of 1 to 5, how well did the cleaner work?

Circle one:
1 Perfectly
2 Good
3 Fair
4 Not at all

Comment: _____

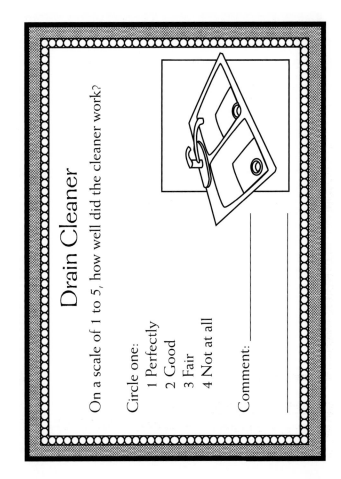

Drain Cleaner

On a scale of 1 to 5, how well did the cleaner work?

Circle one:
1 Perfectly
2 Good
3 Fair
4 Not at all

Comment: _____

Window Cleaner

On a scale of 1 to 5, how well did the cleaner work?

Circle one:
1 Perfectly
2 Good
3 Fair
4 Not at all

Comment: _____

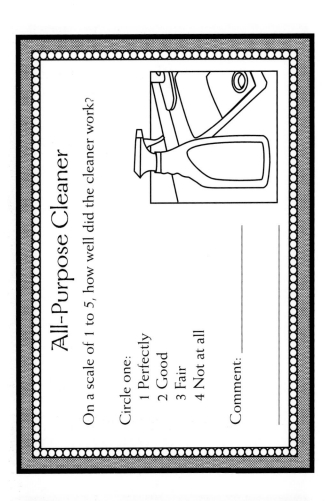

Furniture Polish

On a scale of 1 to 5, how well did the polish work?

Circle one:
1 Perfectly
2 Good
3 Fair
4 Not at all

Comment: _____

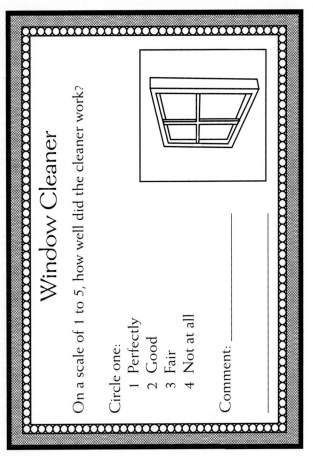

CD-204010 *Taking Godly Care of the Earth*

Idle cars are the devil's workshop

Idling cars waste energy and money. Have students patrol a place where cars often idle, such as the car rider pick-up area at school. Have students cite offenders with tickets. Reproduce these below or have students create their own.

This Is a No Idling Zone.

Car exhaust hurts kids' developing lungs.
Please turn off your engine.

And whosoever shall offend one of these little ones
that believe in me, it is better for him that a millstone were
hanged about his neck, and he were cast into the sea.
Mark 9:42 KJV

This Is a No Idling Zone.

Idling a car for 10 minutes a day adds up to over 60 hours a year.
For an average car, that's 25 gallons of gasoline—wasted!
Please turn off your engine.

"Let nothing be wasted." —Jesus
John 6:12

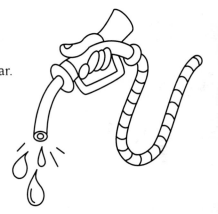

This Is a No Idling Zone.

The earth is the LORD's, and everything in it.
Psalm 24:1

That includes the air that's polluted by idling cars.
Please turn off your engine.

What Would Jesus Drive?

Offer award certificates to drivers who reduce emissions by carpooling or using compact or hybrid cars.

Creation Care Certificate

Carpooling conserves gas and keeps the air clean.

"Well done, good and faithful servant!"
Matthew 25:23

Creation Care Certificate

What would Jesus drive? He did say:
"Let nothing be wasted." John 6:12

IT'S SO COOL TO POOL!

Compact and hybrid cars use less gas and make less pollution.

School's report card

Some state energy offices provide free energy audits that could save your school thousands of dollars. Divide students into the following four groups for a low-tech inspection. Copy the badge patterns (page 38) for children. After students report back with their findings, complete the report cards on pages 39-40 together. Remind students that low grades are okay for the school's first report card—there's lots of opportunity for improvement.

Transportation

Arrange for students to visit several classes to conduct a transportation survey. Have them record the number of car riders, carpoolers, bus riders, and walkers or bikers. They can informally poll students for the reasons behind their transportation choices—for example, would some students be able to walk if there were trails and sidewalks?

Grounds

Have students meet with a grounds custodian and tour the school yard. How often is the lawn mowed? What happens to grass clippings? Are the grounds watered? Does the water come from rain collection barrels or the tap?

Energy

Arrange for students to inspect classrooms, bathrooms, and hallways for open or broken windows, leaky faucets, and running toilets. Check to see if there are lights on in rooms that are not in use.

Cafeteria

Have students visit the cafeteria and find out if any of the food is bought from local farms. What happens to the food waste? Does it go to the dump with the trash? Is it composted? Are washable or disposable items used? Are milk cartons and soda cans recycled?

Reproduce these badges onto heavy paper for students to wear while they perform inspections.

Transportation Officer

_____

Cafeteria Officer

_____

Energy Officer

_____

Grounds Officer

_____

Transportation Report Card

List transportation methods, in order of popularity:

1. _____

2. _____

3. _____

4. _____

Circle grade:

A (most students walk or bike)

B (most students ride the bus)

C (most students carpool)

D (most students are car riders)

Date: _____ Name of School: _____

Signature of transportation officer: _____

Creation Care

Cafeteria Report Card

Give your school one point if the cafeteria:

_____ buys some food from local farmers

_____ composts food waste instead of trashing it

_____ uses metal utensils instead of disposable

_____ recycles soda cans and milk cartons, or reuses drinking glasses

Circle grade:

A (four points)

B (three points)

C (two points)

D (one point)

Date: _____ Name of School: _____

Signature of cafeteria officer: _____

Creation Care

Energy Report Card

Circle grade:

_____ number of broken or open windows

A (only one problem)

_____ number of leaky faucets

B (two problems)

_____ number or running toilets

C (three problems)

_____ number of empty rooms with lights still on

D (four or more problems)

Date: _____ Name of School: _____

Signature of energy officer: _____

Grounds Report Card

Give your school one point if:

Circle grade:

_____ rain water is collected and used for watering

A (four points)

_____ the school yard if made up mostly of natural areas, such as meadow, woodland, or garden

B (three points)

_____ grass clippings are left on the ground or composted with other yard waste

C (two points)

_____ compost or organic fertilizer is used instead of chemicals

D (one point)

Date: _____ Name of School: _____

Signature of grounds officer: _____

Better next time

Use these tips to help students think of ways to improve scores for the next grading period.

Cafeteria

- Help your cafeteria adopt a food waste composting program. Label a trash can "food waste only—no meat," and coordinate with other classes to manage the compost heap.
- Collect utensils and drinking cups from home, garage sales, and flea markets for the cafeteria to use instead of the disposable kind.
- Provide administrators and the school dietician with information about sources for locally-grown produce.

Grounds

- Urge administrators to compost grass clippings and other yard waste, and use organic fertilizer or compost.
- Start a rain collection project using barrels. Call local garden supply centers for supplies.
- Convert lawn to natural meadow, woodland, or gardens; use drought-tolerant shrubs and trees.

Energy

- Report leaky faucets and broken windows
- Learn how to fix running toilets and educate other classes (see diagram at: www.doityourself.com)
- Have one student each day act as the "Light Inspector." During lunch or whenever classrooms are likely to be empty, have the student patrol classrooms and turn off unused lights.
- People need about a gallon of water each day to stay healthy, yet we use 5 gallons every time we flush a toilet. Collect and clean old bricks or big rocks and place them in the tank. These toilet dams reduce the amount of water the toilet uses.

Transportation

- Organize carpool groups by posting a bulletin board in a common area.
- Plan walking and biking trails to nearby neighborhoods. Have students suggest safe routes.
- Install bike racks.

Writing your representative

There's a lot of debate in the United States about land conservation, and we forget that the land doesn't belong to homeowners, businesses, or the government—it only belongs to God. Modern culture tends to give priority to commercial interests—destroying creation for the sake of "the economy." But as Christians, we are told to be "content with what you have" (Hebrews 13:5) God has given us the food, water, and shelter we need: "Is it not enough that you feed on the good pasture? Must you also trample the rest . . . with your feet?" (Ezekiel 34:18). Many government leaders have professed their Christian faith publicly—it's especially important to educate them and hold them accountable. Let students share what they've learned about creation care with their representatives in Congress. Provide copies of the Scripture index on pages 77-79 so that students can support their letters biblically.

PRESIDENT (NAME)
1600 PENNSYLVANIA AVE. NW
WASHINGTON, DC 20500

OFFICE OF SENATOR (NAME)
U.S. SENATOR
WASHINGTON, DC 20510

OFFICE OF REPRESENTATIVE (NAME)
U.S. HOUSE OF REPRESENTATIVES
WASHINGTON, DC 20515

THE RIGHT HONOURABLE (NAME)
PRIME MINISTER OF CANADA
80 WELLINGTON ST.
OTTAWA, ONTARIO K1A0A2

Dear Mr. President
You are the best president
I ever had. I am worried
about the earth where
I live. Rev. Purcell said
God wants us to take
care of it.
So please take care of it.
I hope you win your
election. Love, Bruce

Students may find the names and E-mail addresses of their representatives by calling the U.S. Capitol switchboard at (202) 224-3121 or Canadian offices at 1-800-0-CANADA, or by logging onto *www.senate.gov*, *www.congress.gov*, or *www.canada.gc.ca*.

Help students remember in which legislative district the school is located and the names of their representatives by posting this information in the classroom.

Name _____

Sowing on Good Soil

The land itself must observe a sabbath. . . . Leviticus 25:2
Woe to you who add house to house and join field to field till no space is left and you live alone in the land. Isaiah 5:8

1. What is our modern term for the land's Sabbath, or period of rest?

   _____

2. How can cattle ranchers break the land's Sabbath?

   _____

3. What do you call the natural areas that separate fields of crops?

   _____

4. What happens to soil when fields are joined together without separations?

   _____

5. If we're not farmers, how can we obey God's laws about the land?

   _____

6. Some people think that if we let the land rest or don't use chemical fertilizers, we won't have enough food. Decode to find out what God promises in Leviticus 26:4.

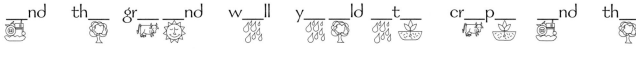

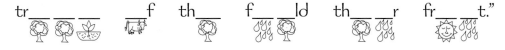

A   E   I   O   U   S

Chapter 4—The other evangelist

*How clearly the sky reveals God's glory! How plainly it shows what he has done!...
No speech or words are used, no sound is heard; yet their message goes out to
all the world and is heard to the ends of the earth.*
Psalm 19:1,3-4 GNT

Before the first missionary, there was the sun, the stars, the thunder clouds—awe-inspiring sights that show the power and love of our Creator. We've all stood on the beach and marveled at the ocean, or studied a seashell's intricate pattern with wonder in our hearts. Isn't God's handiwork glorious?

Even with today's jets and televangelists, the only witness for some people in the world is the splendor of creation—a radiant sunrise or a brilliant nighttime sky. How can we support creation as we would a missionary from our church?

Did you know?

From Mexico City to New Delhi, smog obscures God's glorious sky—usually in poor countries that can't afford clean water, much less "clean-burning" fuels. How does cleaning up pollution help share God's love?

Over 200 years ago, an American Indian named Chased-by-Bears echoed Psalm 19:1 when he said: "When we see the changes of day and night, the sun, the moon, and the stars in the sky . . . anyone must realize that it is the work of someone more powerful than man."

Selected Literature

Still as a Star: A Book of Nighttime Poems by Lee Hopkins: Little Brown, 1989. Well-known poets capture the dreaminess of nighttime.

Sky All Around by Anna Grossnickle Hines: Clarion Books, 1989. Father and daughter look for The Big Dipper, Orion, and other pictures in the nighttime sky.

The Way to Start a Day by Byrd Baylor: Charles Scribner's Sons, 1978. Learn how people around the world celebrate each new sunrise. Afterward, sing *This is the day that the Lord has made. I will rejoice and be glad in it,* from Psalm 118. Encourage students to take in the sensations unique to morning time: dew on the grass and the music of songbirds.

Pollution police

We can look at a busy road and not even see the pollution. But just because we can't see it doesn't mean it's not there. Help students understand pollution by lighting an ordinary candle. There probably won't be much smoke or other visible pollution. Next, hold a glass or white ceramic plate over the candle. After a moment, soot will form on the plate. It is pollution from burning fuel (in this case, the candle wax is the fuel). After the plate cools, allow students to run their fingers through the soot and observe the "dirt" on their fingertip.

Help students think of other ways they can be "pollution police." For example:

You may not see smog in the air, but you may be able to feel it if you're playing or exercising hard outside—for some sensitive people, air pollution can make it difficult to breathe.

You may not be able to tell by looking at a pond, lake, or river whether or not it's contaminated, but dead fish and plants can indicate pollution.

You can't see the chemicals used to treat some lawns and school yards, but they can cause itching, headaches, nausea, and many more serious health problems—especially in pets and children.

End this lesson by reassuring students that they don't have to be afraid of what they can't see or control; they can trust in God and His Word to them which says:

That's right—he rescues you from hidden traps, shields you from deadly hazards. Psalm 91:3 THE MESSAGE

God's ozone versus man's ozone

Do students know that there's "good" ozone and "bad" ozone? Use the worksheet on page 47 to help students understand both. Instruct students to label and color the illustration as you explain it.

Point out the layer of good ozone. Explain that God created good ozone to protect the earth from the sun's harmful rays. Some chemicals we use for air conditioning, refrigeration, and dry cleaning can damage the good ozone, making it thin enough for the sun's harmful rays to get through. These harmful rays damage the earth and peoples' skin.

Show students the pollution that reacts to heat and sunlight to form bad ozone. Explain that people, not God, create bad ozone (also known as smog). When we fill up our gas tanks, the fumes we smell end up as smog. We also make smog by burning fossil fuels like crude oil (gasoline is derived from crude oil). Smog hurts God's entire creation—plants, animals, and people. Only God should make ozone!

Have students research smog levels in different cities. An excellent resource is the EPA's web site, at www.epa.gov/airnow. Students can compare their hometowns to other cities and check out health advisories. (These health advisories are also provided during some weather broadcasts). Use the following chart to help students understand the Air Quality Index.

The **Air Quality Index** (AQI) measures the amount of pollution in the air. People breathe in more air when they're exercising and playing sports, so it's wise to limit heavy-breathing activities outdoors when the air is polluted.

Green (good)
> When the index is green, the air is clean!

Yellow (moderate)
> Very sensitive people (for example, children with asthma) may want to limit strenuous play, exercise, and sports outdoors.

Orange (unhealthy for sensitive groups)
> All adults and children should limit strenuous physical activity outdoors, and people with respiratory or heart disease should avoid strenuous physical activity outdoors.

Red (unhealthy)
> All adults and children should totally avoid physical activity outdoors.

Purple (very unhealthy)
> Adults and children should totally avoid physical activity outdoors.

The American Lung Association says that almost 30 million children are exposed to dangerous levels of smog. Children inhale more air than adults do for their body size and spend more time outdoors, but they are less likely to show symptoms of the damage—even though it causes respiratory infection and decreased lung function later in life.

Name _____

Good Ozone Versus Bad Ozone

Label and color the illustration as your teacher explains it.

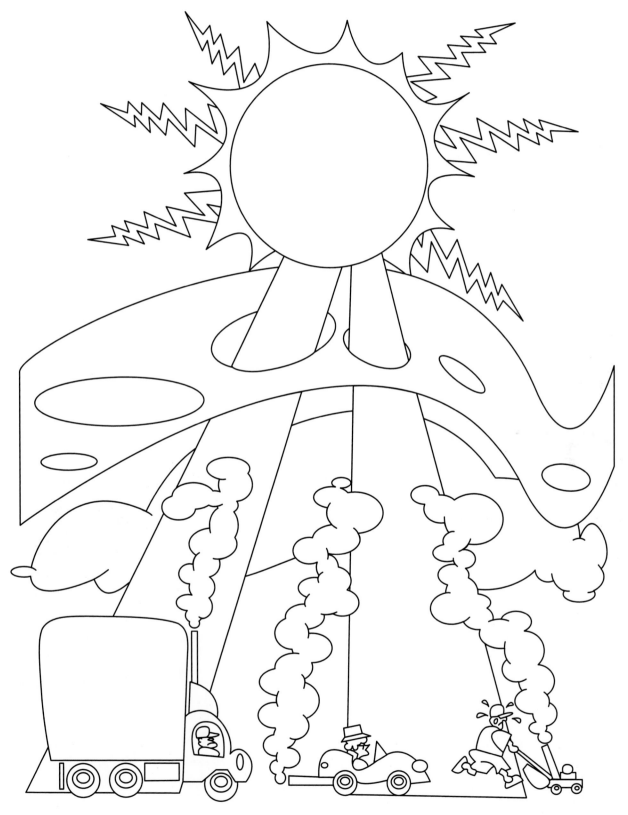

Nature journals

One way we can love creation is by paying attention to it. Remind students of Matthew 6:25-29 NKJV: "Look at the birds…" and "Consider the lilies…". Jesus tells us that we can learn how we should live by observing nature. Have students create journals from used paper. Staple six sheets together, clean sides out, and fold to make a booklet.

Students can use the journals to record their experiences in nature, using pictures and words. Set aside class time to explore outside. Each student should focus on a specific part of God's creation—a dandelion, a pebble, a robin.

Encourage students to use their senses. How many different shades of green are there in the grass? What does sand feel like between your toes? Do buttercups have a scent? How does a honeysuckle taste? What kind of sounds do squirrels make?

Ask students to think about places in nature where they feel close to God, and suggest they find a "prayer closet" outdoors. We think of our church building as God's house, but that's not what Jesus taught. The Bible tells us again and again that God is present in all places to hear our prayers and accept our worship. Solomon knew after he built the Temple that it could not be a dwelling place for God. He said, "Behold, the heaven and the heaven of heavens cannot contain thee, how much less this house that I have builded." (1 Kings 8:27 KJV) Paul preaching in Athens said, "The God who made the world and everything in it is the Lord of heaven and earth and does not live in temples built by hands." (Acts 17:24)

Find inspiration in Psalms 29 and 104. Read these passages with students, and talk about how David praises God by paying attention to His creation.

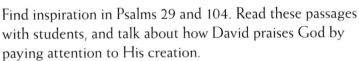

Pen pal project

Set up E-mail correspondence with a class in another country. Your pastor may have contacts at a church or Christian school in another country. The web also has many resources for finding a good match, or you can contact a nation's American embassy to get in touch with an English-speaking school. Students can send descriptions and digital photographs of local flora and fauna, and in return, receive information about exotic environments. E-pals can help students learn about the importance of the natural world in other cultures and religions.

Provide the class with a globe or world map. Get oriented by having students locate the continent, country, and state where you live. Then, have them choose the home of their pen pals. Once the class has voted on a place, discuss what you know about the region's landscape just by looking at the map. The following questions can get students thinking:

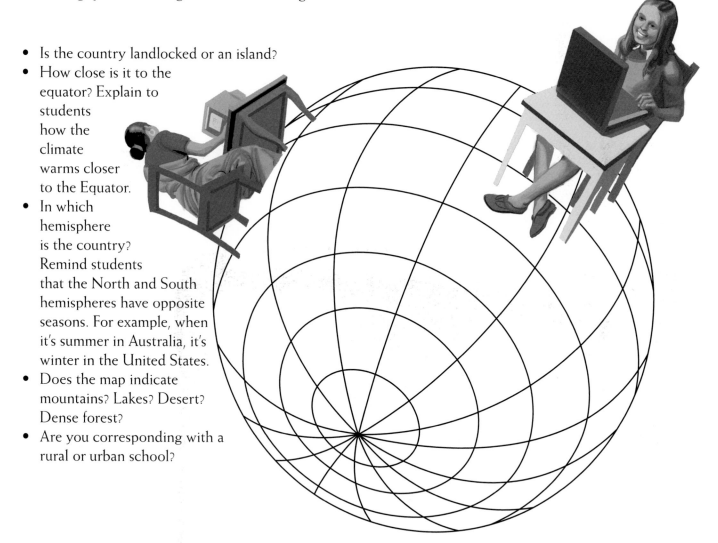

- Is the country landlocked or an island?
- How close is it to the equator? Explain to students how the climate warms closer to the Equator.
- In which hemisphere is the country? Remind students that the North and South hemispheres have opposite seasons. For example, when it's summer in Australia, it's winter in the United States.
- Does the map indicate mountains? Lakes? Desert? Dense forest?
- Are you corresponding with a rural or urban school?

Take a field trip to the zoo, paying special attention to the area devoted to your pen pals' region. For example, if are you corresponding with a class from Botswana, visit the African habitat. Afterward, the class can E-mail pen pals their observations and ask questions. How is the zoo different from the real thing?

Life cycle of blue jeans

All of us are guilty of buying things and then later getting rid of them, without ever thinking of the environmental or human toll involved. For instance, take your everyday pair of blue jeans. Poll students: how many are wearing them? Ask students to think about the life cycle of the jeans. Use the worksheet on page 51 to guide them through the process—from cotton field to the dump.

Fashion for creation

Who said fashion can't glorify God? (Remind students of Genesis 3:21, where God made clothes for Adam and Eve!) Plan a "Clothes for Creation" fashion show. Students can bring in items they've outgrown to trade with other students. The goal is for each student to have a new outfit for the fashion show. Block off a "runway" area, with seating on either side. Invite other classes, and provide snacks and fun music. Take pictures so that the class can put together a "fashion magazine" later. Have students prepare a short script beforehand, and take turns introducing each other. For example:

"Nichole is sporting an orchid-colored parka and funky boots—a look she says was inspired by the rain forest. By not buying her parka at the mall, Nichole saved a pound of chemicals from polluting creation!"

Name _____

Life Cycle of Blue Jeans

Match the following facts to the number of the corresponding illustration.

A. _____ Getting jeans from the factory to your closet uses up a lot of fuel. Fifty percent of all pollution is automobile exhaust.

B. _____ Twenty-five percent of all pesticides are used for growing cotton. Most cotton is grown in poor, hungry countries, and uses fertile land where they could grow food.

C. _____ The toxins used to make blue dye pollute the environment, and machines use polluting chemicals to spin and weave the cotton.

D. _____ Jeans and other clothes are usually sewn in poor countries where the labor is cheap, or in illegal factories in America. Sometimes children are employed, working long hours in unsafe conditions.

E. _____ Most people get rid of their jeans when they outgrow them or they're no longer the latest style, and the jeans end up in the landfill.

F. _____ Pumice used for "stone washing" and copper used for rivets and fastenings destroys the land where it is mined.

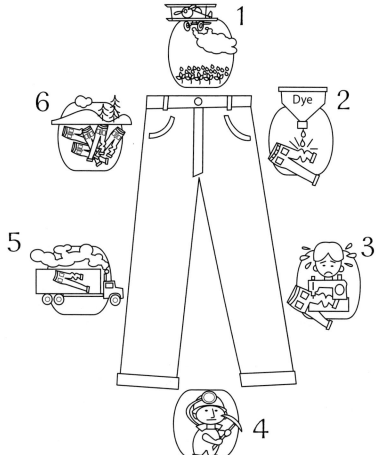

Bonus
Think about the life cycles of other everyday items, and the effects they have on creation.

Fashion magazine

Give students a piece of paper and a picture of themselves on the runway. Have students glue the picture to the paper, and then decorate the page. (Or, students can scan the images and create an E-zine.) They can write their name and fun facts like, "Hairstyle by Jordania" or "When Chris isn't modeling, he enjoys playing soccer and hanging out with his friends at Grace Church."

Include a note at the beginning of the magazine that explains the project: "Ms. Brooks' 2nd grade class dresses for success! Instead of throwing out our old clothes, we brought them to school to share with other students. We've learned that recycling clothes is an important way to take care of God's creation." Include a few scriptural references and facts about how new clothes hurt the environment. Staple the pages together or have them bound at a copy shop. Display the magazine in the school library.

Name _____

The Heavens Need Our Help!

Choose the correct word from the word bank to fill in the blank.

1. Natural gas, coal, and oil are _____ _____. People burn them for heat, for cooking, and for powering cars.

2. _____ _____ _____ is created by people from car exhaust and gas fumes. It hurts plants and animals, and causes people to have trouble breathing. It is especially bad in _____ cities.

3. Another name for ground-level ozone is _____, which forms when sunlight mixes with pollution.

4. Good _____ was created by God to protect the earth from the sun's harmful rays. People can destroy it by using air conditioning, refrigerators, and dry cleaning.

5. Jesus tells us to _____ the lilies. They don't go shopping or worry about how they look—and they're "dressed" better than any fashion model! Jesus tells us we can learn how to live our own lives by _____ _____ to His _____.

The earth is full of the goodness of the Lord.

Psalms 33:5

Word Bank
smog
ozone
ground-level ozone
consider
fossil fuels
creation
paying attention
poor

CD-204010 *Taking Godly Care of the Earth*

Chapter 5—Outdoor learning

*But ask the animals, and they will teach you, or the birds of the air, and they will tell you;
or speak to the earth, and it will teach you, or let the fish of the sea inform you.*

Job 12:7-8

Even though everyday contact with creation is one of the most important parts of a Christian education, Christian school yards often look a lot like public and secular school yards—chemically-treated lawn and playing fields, plastic play sets, huge parking lots, and decorative trees or shrubs here or there. Educators are discovering that students learn more and are healthier in the "outdoor classroom." The Bible tells us that creation offers this and even more for our children. The following activities can make your school yard a place that restores and glorifies God's handiwork and nurtures students' appreciation of creation.

Did you know?

You can make a difference! Consider leading your school in a long-term commitment to creation-minded landscaping. Fruit trees, wildlife habitats, pergolas, fountains, and other features can transform a barren lot into a garden worthy of King Solomon—usually for less than the cost of manufactured play equipment and lawn maintenance.

Selected Literature

The Tiny Seed by Eric Carle: Picture Book Studio, 1987. Dazzling collage illustrations tell the story of a flower's life cycle. Complement this story with Jesus' parables about seeds in Matthew 13.

Don't Worry About Tomorrow (Just Like Jesus Said) by Melody Carlson: Broadman and Holman Publishers, 2002. A nice lesson in contentment.

Ox-Cart Man by Donald Hall: Viking Press, 1979. An early American family works and lives in harmony with the seasons.

School gardens

Even a small garden takes a lot of work, but the rewards are great. Parents can help by volunteering on planting day (have one adult for every 7 students), lending tools, or donating seedlings or clippings. Promote a feeling of ownership by involving students throughout the process. Keep the garden a manageable and enjoyable size. Choose a theme (see pages 56-57) and discuss what your garden needs to grow: sun, water, and good soil. Then scout the perfect spot. Help students with this checklist:

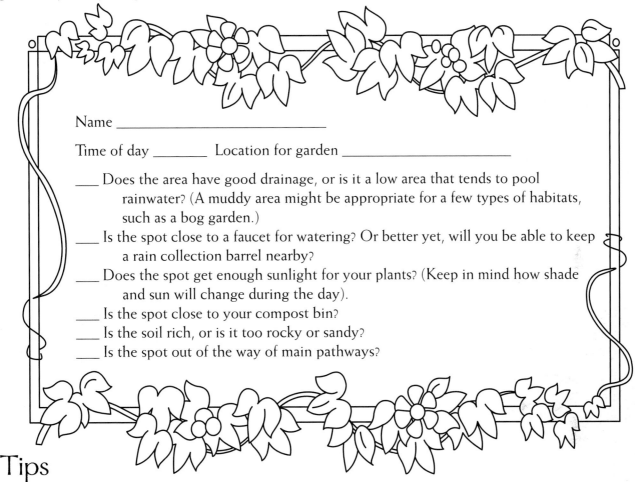

Name _____

Time of day _____ Location for garden _____

___ Does the area have good drainage, or is it a low area that tends to pool rainwater? (A muddy area might be appropriate for a few types of habitats, such as a bog garden.)

___ Is the spot close to a faucet for watering? Or better yet, will you be able to keep a rain collection barrel nearby?

___ Does the spot get enough sunlight for your plants? (Keep in mind how shade and sun will change during the day).

___ Is the spot close to your compost bin?

___ Is the soil rich, or is it too rocky or sandy?

___ Is the spot out of the way of main pathways?

Tips

- Plan ahead! Several months before planting season, cover the area with a thick layer of newspapers or black plastic; weight down with stones. Grass and weeds will decompose to enrich the soil.

- Use a seed catalog for pictures and information, but work with small plants to see quicker results. Keep in mind which plants will tolerate your climate at the time of year you'll be gardening.

- Make the most of children's natural interests—provide students with kid-size tools, let them play with the hose while they water, reward the student who picks the weed with the longest roots.

- Have students make garden markers using scraps of cardboard, and keep a calendar updated with garden news. For example, "September 5: Lavender is the winner! It is the first plant to flower!"

- Remember to use absolutely no chemicals in a children's garden. Start building up compost for fertilizer a few months before planting time. (See page 15 for composting instructions.) Instead of using pesticides, pick off bugs by hand and put them in a bucket of water. Use this time to learn about beneficial and harmful insects (page 20). Herbs, marigolds, onions, and garlic also help keep bugs away.

Rainbow garden

Choose from zinnias, goldenrod, cornflowers, petunias, begonias, and many others to create a colorful arc of flowers. Plant "clouds" of white impatiens at either end of the rainbow. Bright flowers attract butterflies, hummingbirds, and other critters—a great reminder of God's covenant with every living creature!

Council ring

A seating area will make it easier to have class outdoors. Using natural materials such as stones or logs, create a circle of seats. Pick a spot that is at least partially shaded for warmer months. Use the area for worship, prayer, story time, or messy science experiments.

Bible garden

With grapevines, anise, coriander, cumin, hyssop, dill, mustard, cucumbers, leeks, and onions—even reeds and bulrushes—students can experience sights, tastes, and smells from the Bible first-hand.

Pizza garden

Students can create a pie-shaped garden divided into "slices" of tomatoes, oregano, basil, and onions. Buon appetito!

CD-204010 *Taking Godly Care of the Earth*

American Indian garden

American Indians are known for understanding God through creation. Plant pumpkin, beans, squash, and corn and learn about their traditional uses. A Dakota Sioux named Zitkala-Sa said: "The voice of the Great Spirit is heard in the twittering of birds, the rippling of mighty waters, and the sweet breathing of flowers." Encourage students to hear God in their garden.

Sunflower garden

Enjoy watching a giant flower grow from a tiny seed. Compare the size of sunflower seeds to a mustard seed, and read Jesus' parable together (Mark 4:31-32). Sunflowers grow quickly, so measure them weekly. Have students compare their height to the tall blooms'. When birds begin to peck at the seeds, students can enjoy a tasty snack, too.

Habitat garden

Design a home for wildlife. Create a toad abode from a simple clay pot and saucer, or place large rocks in direct sunlight for a lizard lounge. Contact the National Wildlife Federation Schoolyard Habitat program for more detailed instructions. Students can even get their habitat certified!

For God so loved the world . . .

As children, many of us learned John 3:16 as an easy formula for getting into heaven. In doing so, we ignore the importance of the first six words. "World" does not just refer to humankind—it's translated from the Greek word for cosmos, or the entire universe that God created in harmony. As a daily reminder of God's love for the whole universe, write John 3:16 on the chalkboard. Every morning, have students substitute a different word in place of "world" that describes God's creation.

Dandelion safari

Want to get students learning outside today, but all you have to work with is grass and or a parking lot? Make friends with a manicured lawn's worst enemy: the dandelion. Learn about the life cycle of plants by observing this familiar flower.

Dandelions grow fast. Place an old ruler by one to chart its growth. Talk about the dandelion's different stages:

1. Early in the spring, dandelions sprout and flower. Blooms close up at night and on cloudy days. Cover the flower with a bucket to demonstrate.

2. After the flower has been pollinated, it no longer needs the bright yellow petals to attract insects. The bloom closes up.

3. Seeds develop within the closed head, and within a few days it will open into a fluffy ball. Wind blows the seeds, which are each equipped with a feathery parachute! Observe a seed through a magnifying glass. Have students note the tiny burrs that will help anchor the seed to the ground wherever it lands.

Explain to students that dandelions can "take over" a lawn because they use a lot of food and water—but dandelions are useful, too. The roots can be roasted and ground to make dandelion tea. Dandelion flowers are used for making wine. And early in the spring, some people pick the tender, young leaves and toss them in a salad. For more fun, read *Hello, dandelions!* by Barbara Williams.

Knock-knock, is anybody home?

Trees take care of creation, too! They keep our air clean by taking in carbon dioxide and giving off oxygen. Trees also provide homes for other plants and animals. Take the class outside to a forest or wooded area, and enjoy these tree activities first-hand. Afterward, share special findings with the rest of this class.

In late summer you can hear the humming songs of cicadas, or locusts. In the fall, look for their brown discarded skins.

Do you see any bird or squirrel nests in the branches?

Check the leaves for caterpillars, insect larva, walking sticks, aphids, and bees.

Examine the bark carefully for spiders, flies, ants, beetles, and moths. Peek behind the bark, too. Look carefully—the colors and markings of some critters blend in, hiding them from enemies.

Look around the roots for earthworms, slugs, and snails. Do you see any sign of tunneling chipmunks, mice, rabbits, or moles?

To be called a "tree hugger" is sometimes used as an insult. But the Bible tells us that we should strive to be more like trees! Have students take their Bibles and pencils outside to complete the worksheet on page 60. Each student can pick a tree to investigate. Encourage touching, listening, smelling, and careful examination.

Name _____

Proud to Be Like a Poplar Tree

Answer the questions and think about what people have in common with trees.

1. What do both you and the tree need in order to survive?

   _____

2. Look at your body and compare it to the tree. Our skin protects us from germs. What part of the tree protects it?

   _____

3. We stand with out feet planted on the ground. What part of a tree keeps it attached to the ground?

   _____

4. The part of our body that helps us stand tall and straight is called the "trunk." Label the tree's trunk and the person's trunk.

5. A tree uses its branches to reach up and "grab" sunlight. What parts of our bodies are like a tree's branches?

   _____

I will pour out my Spirit on your offspring,
and my blessing on your descendants.
They will spring up like grass in a meadow,
like poplar trees by flowing streams.
Isaiah 44:3-4

CD-204010 *Taking Godly Care of the Earth*

Outdoor Bible Study

Head outside with your Bibles and find out what God's Word has to say about cedars, palms, mighty oaks, and poplar trees. Have student volunteers look up these groups of verses to read for the class, and then use the discussion questions or activities that follow each set of verses.

Your children will grow like a tree in the grass. They will be like poplar trees growing beside streams of water.
Isaiah 44:4 NCV

But I am like an olive tree flourishing in the house of God; I trust in God's unfailing love for ever and ever. Psalm 52:8

Good people will prosper like palm trees.
Psalm 92:12 THE MESSAGE

If you have a stream nearby, point out how lush and green the plants are that grow beside it.

Think about the type of climate where you find palm trees—there is plenty of rain and warm sun. God gives trees just what they need to grow.

Read on in Psalm 92 to find out why the palm tree flourishes—to show that the Lord is good. How does a healthy palm tree show the Lord's goodness? How can a tree trust in God's mercy? We don't think of trees as having emotions or being aware of things like people are, but they trust God, too—for food, water, and what else?

Burst into song, you mountains, you forests and all your trees! Isaiah 44:23

Let the fields be jubilant, and everything in them. Then all the trees of the forest will sing for joy. Psalm 96:12

Praise the LORD . . . you mountains and all hills, fruit trees and all cedars. Psalm 148:7-9

What sounds do you hear in the forest? Birds in the branches? Wind through the leaves? How does a tree sing praise to God?

Each tree is recognized by its own fruit. People do not pick figs from thornbushes, or grapes from briers. Luke 6:44

The fruit of the Spirit is love, joy, peace, patience, kindness, goodness, faithfulness, gentleness and self-control. Galatians 5:22-23

If you see apples on a tree, you know it's an apple tree. God tells us that it's the same with people. We are judged by our "fruit." We can think of ourselves as a beautiful apple tree, but if sour lemons are hanging from our branches, we're not an apple tree!

What is something loving, kind, or gentle you've done today? What sort of tree does this make you?

Name _____

Reap Life Everlasting!

Choose the correct word from the word and definition bank to complete the Bible verses.

praise	to express respect and appreciation
fruit	the part of a plant that contains seeds, it's usually sweet and can be eaten
seeds	eggs from a plant, fertilized with pollen, that can grow into a new plant
world	the cosmos or universe, the system of order and harmony that God created out of nothing

1. For God so loved the _____ that he gave his one and only Son. (John 3:16)

2. The _____ of the Spirit is love, joy, peace, patience, kindness, goodness, faithfulness, gentleness and self-control. (Galatians 5:22-23)

3. _____ the Lord . . . you mountains and all hills, fruit trees and all cedars. (Psalm 148:7-9)

4. For as the soil makes the sprout come up and a garden causes _____ to grow, so the Sovereign LORD will make righteousness and praise spring up before all nations. (Isaiah 61:11)

CD-204010 *Taking Godly Care of the Earth*

Chapter 6—Our neighbors in the rainforest

"A new command I give you: Love one another. As I have loved you, so you must love one another.
By this all men will know that you are my disciples, if you love one another."

John 13:34

Students are probably already aware that rainforests are home to millions of plants and animals, and that they are being destroyed at an alarming rate. God holds us accountable for "every animal that moves on the face of the Earth," and the rainforests are home to half of these animals!

Taking care of the rainforests is also a way to show our love for the people who live there. The choices we make everyday affect whether they have food, shelter, and clean water. This chapter will help students understand the connection between caring for the Earth and Jesus' command to love one another.

Did you know?

Compare world maps with a globe. Have students observe how the three-dimensional globe must be distorted when it's converted into a two-dimensional map. Which continents become bigger or smaller? How might the distortion affect our view of these areas?

We used to call rainforest areas "jungles." Ask students to think about the difference between the two names, and discuss how connotations can affect word meanings. What are some other terms that have become "politically incorrect"? Can this sort of sensitivity be a good thing? What does Proverbs 13:3 say about guarding our lips?

Selected Literature

My Side of the Mountain by Jean Craighead George: Penguin, 1998. Newberry award-winning tale of a city boy who decides to live off the land.

The Lorax by Dr. Suess: Random House, 1971. Older students can enjoy thinking about this classic's environmental metaphors—it's appropriate for tree huggers of all ages.

Echoes for the Eye by Barbara Juster Esbensen: HarperCollins, 1996. Poems help students discover patterns in nature. You'll never look at a storm, leaf, or honeycomb the same way again.

My neighborhood is huge!

On a city map, have students point out where they live. Who are their neighbors? Next door? The entire street? Inform students that Jesus gave us a different definition for the word "neighbor." To find it, read the story of the traveling Samaritan (Luke 10:25-37). Our neighbor is anyone who is in need, not necessarily someone who lives close by.

Explain how Jesus' audience felt about the Samaritans—they couldn't stand them! They looked different and had a different religion. No one would give a Samaritan the time of day. Yet Jesus tells his audience to be more like the Samaritan!

The Samaritans from Jesus' time still live today—many in Palestinian communities. But in the story, Samaritans stand for anyone we dislike or ignore. Who do we dislike or ignore today?

Because America has more food and medicine than most other countries, the vast majority of sick and hungry people live in other places. We are called to be good neighbors and show mercy to people in need all over the world!

Using a globe, point out where some of the world's poorest people live: in the tropical rainforests near the Equator. Have students pick a rainforest country they've never heard of—Chad, Guinea, Cambodia, Guyana, Suriname, etc. Remind them that the people who live there are our neighbors, too. Using an almanac, get to know your new neighbors! What's the country's population? Language? Exports? Geography? Culture? Animals? Ethnic groups? Prayer needs?

 CD-204010 *Taking Godly Care of the Earth*

Jesus is here?

What if Jesus were planning a visit to your classroom today? How would students prepare? Have them think of all the nice things they'd do for Him.

If Jesus got chilly, who would give Him her favorite sweater?

If Jesus were hungry, who would give Him his lunch money?

If Jesus were sick in the nurse's office, who would skip recess to visit Him?

If kids were making fun of Jesus, who would stand up and defend Him?

Students will answer the above questions with an enthusiastic, "Me! Me!"

Now, reveal to students that Jesus has been at school! Just yesterday you saw some students making fun of Jesus, and not one person helped Him. And yesterday, Jesus had to go home sick. Did anybody visit Him after school? As students express disbelief, read Matthew 25:31-46. Jesus tells us that whenever we feed a hungry person, or visit a sick person, or care for anyone who is ignored and overlooked, it's just like we are doing it for Jesus Himself!

Disciple Detectives

"A new command I give you: Love one another. As I have love you, so you must love one another."
John 13:34

Use the following true/false quiz to help students understand the command Jesus gives His followers in John 13:34. What signs show others that we are Jesus' disciples?

Disciples of Jesus get good grades.

Disciples of Jesus go to church every Sunday.

Disciples of Jesus have the nicest things—a big house, new clothes, and cool toys.

Disciples of Jesus are good at sports.

Disciples of Jesus have the most friends.

Disciples of Jesus never get sad or angry.

Disciples of Jesus don't get sick.

Disciples of Jesus serve other people.

Only for the last question is the answer always "true." Explain to students that disciples can get good grades, go to church, have a lot of friends, etc., but Jesus tells us one sure way to show that we're Christians: to serve and love others like He did.

Feet washing

Materials: Water and washcloths, towels for drying, flip-flops

On a warm day, have students wear flip flops to school. Offer a prize for the student who returns from recess with the dirtiest feet.

When even the daintiest little toes are covered with grime, gather students together to read John 13 and discover what it means to love Jesus' way. How did Jesus show perfect love, the greatest love of all? With a brilliant sermon? A heavenly display of fireworks?

No, Jesus showed us how to love by washing His disciples' feet! Imagine how dirty and blistered their feet were—walking in the dust all day in sandals, with sand, mud, animal droppings, and sharp rocks! Only servants or slaves would have had such a nasty job.

Pair students together and have them wash each others' feet. Afterward, talk about how serving other people shows that we're Jesus' disciples. Today we have socks, sneakers, and showers, and we don't need servants to wash our feet. What are other ways we can show Jesus' love? Help student get started with these ideas for serving others:

- Picking up litter in an under-served neighborhood
- Helping elderly neighbors with yard and house work
- Taking care of friends or siblings when they're sick
- Volunteering with parents at a homeless shelter
- Cleaning out the kitchen cupboard for a local food pantry

The drive-thru rainforest

The rainforest is not as far away as we might think! In fact, it's as close as our next meal! Use these illustrations to show the connection between the rainforest and what we eat. Reproduce for students to color, cut apart and put in order.

1

Fifty-five square feet of Rainforest,
about the size of a small kitchen,
can have over 10 different species of trees.

2

Fifty-five square feet of rainforest are
destroyed every second for cattle pasture.

3

One-third of the world's grain is fed to cattle
and other livestock. That's enough to give
every man, woman, and child a meal a day.

4

Burned or over-grazed land turns into desert.
Because mosquito and rat populations increase,
people living nearby become infected with
malaria and other diseases.

 CD-204010 *Taking Godly Care of the Earth*

Have students color the drawings with markers or colored pencils, and staple them together into a booklet. Students can keep the booklet in the car to encourage them not to ask for a burger every time they see golden arches on the highway.

5

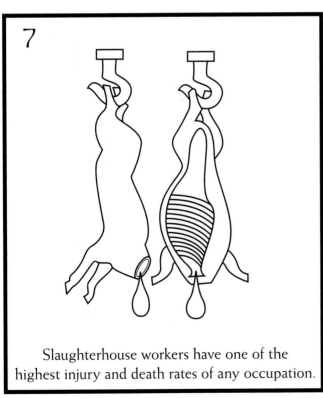

When rainforests are destroyed,
plants that could be used to make medicine
become extinct.

6

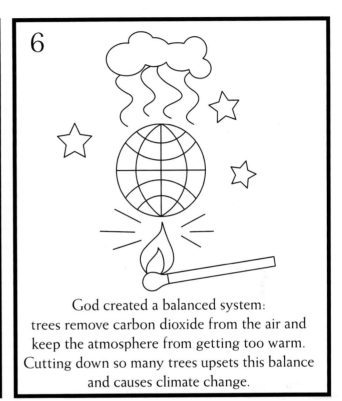

God created a balanced system:
trees remove carbon dioxide from the air and
keep the atmosphere from getting too warm.
Cutting down so many trees upsets this balance
and causes climate change.

7

Slaughterhouse workers have one of the
highest injury and death rates of any occupation.

8

Fifty-five square feet of rainforest can produce
one hamburger. Try ordering a meal without any
beef, or eat at home and donate your change to a
Central or South American rainforest preservation
or relief group. For the price of a fast food meal, a
third world family could eat for several days.

The rainforest deserves a break today!

"Don't become so well-adjusted to your culture that you fit into it without even thinking." Romans 12:2 THE MESSAGE

Begin by having students think about Romans 12:2 (above). When we watch television, are we zoned out, or do we pay attention and think about the messages we're seeing and hearing?

Materials: Television, VCR, towel

Many fast food restaurants in the United States buy cheap rainforest beef to make hamburgers. These restaurants target children with sophisticated marketing, including toy promotions, playgrounds, and television advertising. Teaching students how to evaluate fast food advertising is the first step in helping them make decisions based on God's Word—not the world's. Record a fast food commercial that appears during children's programming and show it in class.

Use the pause and mute features to focus students' attention on specific elements. Emphasize the sound track by draping the screen with a towel.

Discussion questions:

- What's the commercial about? What happens in this 30-second story?

- What about the commercial appeals to kids? Parents?

- Advertisers have found that children are loyal to brands that use themes of patriotism and good health. Point out children playing sports and other physical activity that has nothing to do with the food. Can students spot a national flag in the background? Listen closely, is there a patriotic melody woven into the sound track?

- Is there food in the commercial? Ask students if the food they've eaten at the restaurant looks like it does in the commercial. Since real food doesn't photograph well, what substitutes may they have used? Have students use their imaginations—glass ice cubes? Cardboard French fries? Plastic lettuce glistening with baby oil?

- Do students notice other tricks? Are toys talking? Do celebrities really eat there all the time?

- What's the purpose of the commercial? If the company's ultimate goal is to make money, is this compatible with our Christian values? (See Matthew 6:24)

- Why does the commercial not mention rainforests or cattle ranching? What else do they leave out? (For example, how their high-fat and high-sugar foods contribute to high rates of obesity and diabetes in children).

Homework

Kids may not be able to fix a hole in the ozone or clean up the water supply in Eritrea, but they do have a lot of power in the American fast food industry. Parents may pay and provide transportation, but kids are the real buyers. Help students understand the choices they have—they can help sell fast food by nagging their parents for it, or they can be obedient—to their parents and to God. Copy pages 72-73 for each student to make into a booklet to keep track of how much or how little they choose to ask for fast food.

Long-distance fruit (page 74 worksheet)

Tropical rainforests are often destroyed to grow oranges, pineapples, bananas, and other fruits. The worksheet on page 74 will help students understand where many common fruits originate, and the consequences of their choices in the grocery store. Copy the worksheet and have students take it to the grocery store to check the stickers. (Students could also bring stickers from home to place on a world map in the classroom.)

Discuss alternatives to tropical produce.
(Farmers' markets for locally grown fruits, home-grown, buy fruit in season, etc.)

Discuss the advantages of getting fruit from rainforest areas.
(You can get it year-round and it sometimes costs less.)

Discuss the disadvantages of rainforest area fruit.
(Rainforest has to be destroyed to grow the fruit; it has to travel a long way to get to my grocery store, it doesn't taste as fresh, and it takes a lot of fuel to get it here.)

Dear Parents:

As part of our creation stewardship studies, students are learning how their everyday choices can help or hurt the rainforest. Acres of rainforests are cleared every minute in Central and South America for cattle ranching, and many fast food restaurants in the United States buy this cheap beef for hamburgers.

These restaurants target your child, considering him or her a surrogate salesman. This booklet allows your son or daughter to keep track of their own "sales techniques." For the next two weeks, please use this booklet to hold your student accountable for each fast food request.

You may supplement our lesson at home by limiting television time, analyzing fast food advertisements with your child, and checking together for "USA-bred" labels on beef in the grocery store. Let's help our students make decisions based on God's Word—not the fast food industry!

Students may use the following requesting styles alone or in combination, but usually stick to the one or two that work best. Students will place a check on the pages if they choose to use one of the techniques.

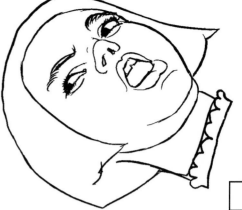

Forceful request with subtle threat:

"Dad would take me."

Check and date a box if you used this technique.

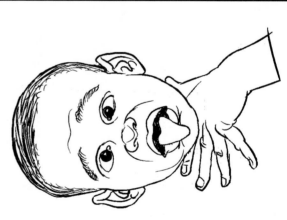

Threatening request:

"That other food will make me sick!"

Check and date a box if you used this technique.

Children, obey your parents in the Lord: for this is right.
Ephesians 6:1 KJV

Persistent request:

"I'm gonna ask just one more time!"

Check and date a box if you used this technique.

☐ ☐ ☐ ☐

Pleading request with pity threat:

"Please! Everybody will make fun of me if I bring juice in a thermos!"

Check and date a box if you used this technique.

☐ ☐ ☐ ☐

Demonstrative request:

Tantrum with tears…

Check and date a box if you used this technique.

☐ ☐ ☐ ☐

Sugar-coated request:

"You're the best dad in the whole world!"

Check and date a box if you used this technique.

☐ ☐ ☐ ☐

Name _____

Long-Distance Fruit

Name of grocery store:_____

Circle season: winter   spring   summer   fall

TYPE OF FRUIT	WHERE IS IT GROWN?
Bananas	_____
Blueberries	_____
Coconuts	_____
Grapes	_____
Kiwis	_____
Lemons	_____
Limes	_____
Mangoes	_____
Oranges	_____
Papayas	_____
Pineapples	_____
Raspberries	_____
Other fruit	_____

CD-204010 *Taking Godly Care of the Earth*

Name _____

Fruit Family History

Today we get some of our oranges from Central and South American rainforests. They're inexpensive and available year-round. Generations ago, oranges were a special treat. Talk with your grandparents or another older adult about differences in the food they ate growing up and the food that's available now.

Adult's name:_____   Adult's year of birth:_____

1. When they were my age, they usually ate these foods:

    _____

2. They got most of their food from (circle one):

    the store   their family's own garden or farm

    restaurants   other:

3. Their favorite foods growing up were: _____

4. I usually eat these foods: _____

5. I get most of my food from (circle one):

    the store   their family's own garden or farm

    restaurants   other:

6. My favorite food is: _____

7. Here's something interesting I found about how people used to eat:

    _____

Name _____

To Sum It All Up . . .

Unscramble each word and then match the corresponding letters to the complete the Bible verse.

NDOMACM .... to give orders to   __ __ __ __ __ __ __

BRGOHIEN .... a person who lives nearby,   __ __ __ __ __ __ __ __
                        or a person in need   8   10 11 12
                        anywhere in the world

TOPERX .... to sell items to other   __ __ __ __ __ __
                          countries

ZERAG .... to feed on grass in a pasture   __ __ __ __ __
                                                             7 13

ISPCLIED .... one of Jesus' companions,   __ __ __ __ __ __ __
                           anyone who helps spread   14   1
                           Jesus' teachings

OFTADEOISTNER .... clearing away all the trees   __ __ __ __ __ __ __ __ __ __ __ __
                                                           15   4   9

ELGJUN .... a tangled mass of tropical   __ __ __ __ __ __
                           vegetation   6

NOTAOONNITC ...... a suggested or implied   __ __ __ __ __ __ __ __ __ __
                     meaning of a word   2

The entire law is summed up in a single command:

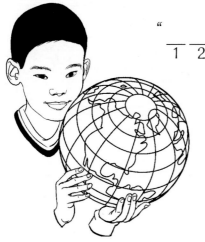

" __ __ V __   __ Y __ __   __ __ __ __ __ __ __ __
  1 2   4   2 6 7   8 4 9 10 11 12 2 7

                                                    "
  __ __   __ Y __ __ __ __ __ __.
  13 14   2 6 7 14 4 1 15

Galatians 5:14

SCRIPTURE INDEX

Chapter 1—Our first responsibility

Theme verse

*God spoke: "Let us make human beings in our image, make them reflecting our nature
So they can be responsible for the fish in the sea, the birds in the air, the cattle,
And, yes, Earth itself, and every animal that moves on the face of Earth."*
Genesis 1:26 THE MESSAGE

Chapter verses

But [He] made himself nothing, taking the very nature of a servant. Philippians 2:7

GOD took the Man and set him down in the Garden of Eden to work the ground and keep it in order.
Genesis 2:15 THE MESSAGE

And God saw that it was good. Genesis 1:10

"Let nothing be wasted." John 6:12

"Nothing will be impossible for you." Matthew 17:20

. . . on the outside you appear to people as righteous but on the inside you are full of hypocrisy and wickedness. Matthew 23:28

Chapter 2—The rainbow covenant

Theme Verse

*"Whenever the rainbow appears in the clouds, I will see it and remember the everlasting
covenant between God and all living creatures of every kind on the earth."*
Genesis 9:16

Chapter Verses

He replied, "When evening comes, you say, 'It will be fair weather, for the sky is red,' and in the morning, 'Today it will be stormy, for the sky is red and overcast.' You know how to interpret the appearance of the sky, but you cannot interpret the signs of the times." Matthew 16:2-3

"Let nothing be wasted." John 6:12

"Once again, the kingdom of heaven is like a net that was let down into the lake and caught all kinds of fish." Matthew 13:47

As Jesus walked beside the Sea of Galilee, he saw Simon and his brother Andrew casting a net into the lake, for they were fishermen. Mark 1:16

Whenever the rainbow appears in the clouds, I will see it and remember the everlasting covenant between God and all living creatures of every kind on the earth." Genesis 9:16

Chapter Passages

Genesis 9:12-17

John 6:1-14

Matthew 17:24-27

Luke 1:5-11

 CD-204010 *Taking Godly Care of the Earth*

Chapter 3—Whose Earth is it, anyway?

Theme Verse

The earth is the LORD's, and everything in it, the world, and all who live in it.
Psalm 24:1

Chapter Verses

"His master replied, 'Well done, good and faithful servant!" Matthew 25:21

"The land must not be sold permanently, because the land is mine and you are but aliens and my tenants." Leviticus 25:23

Woe to you who add house to house and join field to field till no space is left and you live alone in the land. Isaiah 5:8

And whosoever shall offend one of these little ones that believe in me, it is better for him that a millstone were hanged about his neck, and he were cast into the sea. Mark 9:42 KJV

"Let nothing be wasted." John 6:12

"Well done, good and faithful servant! Matthew 25:23

Don't be obsessed with getting more material things. Be relaxed with what you have. Since God assured us, "I'll never let you down, never walk off and leave you." Hebrews 13:5 THE MESSAGE

Is it not enough for you to feed on the good pasture? Must you also trample the rest of your pasture with your feet? Is it not enough for you to drink clear water? Must you also muddy the rest with your feet? Ezekiel 34:18

"Speak to the Israelites and say to them: 'When you enter the land I am going to give you, the land itself must observe a sabbath to the LORD. Leviticus 25:2

"I will send you rain in its season and the ground will yield its crops and the trees of the field their fruit." Leviticus 26:4

Chapter Passages

Leviticus 25, 26

Matthew 25:14-30

Chapter 4—The other evangelist

Theme Verse

How clearly the sky reveals God's glory! How plainly it shows what he has done!…
No speech or words are used, no sound is heard; yet their message goes out to all the world and is heard to the ends of the earth.
Psalm 19:1,3-4 GNT

Chapter Verses

That's right—he rescues you from hidden traps, shields you from deadly hazards. Psalm 91:3 THE MESSAGE

But will God indeed dwell on the earth? behold, the heaven and heaven of heavens cannot contain thee; how much less this house that I have builded? 1 Kings 8:27 KJV

The God who made the world and everything in it is the Lord of heaven and earth, and does not live in temples built by hands. Acts 17:24

The LORD God made garments of skin for Adam and his wife and clothed them. Genesis 3:21

Chapter Passages

Matthew 6:25-29

Psalms 29, 104

Chapter 5—Outdoor learning

Theme Verse

But ask the animals, and they will teach you, or the birds of the air, and they will tell you;
or speak to the earth, and it will teach you, or let the fish of the sea inform you.
Job 12:7-8

Chapter Verses

For God so loved the world that he gave his one and only Son, that whoever believes in him shall not perish but have eternal life. John 3:16

Your children will grow like a tree in the grass. They will be like poplar trees growing beside streams of water. Isaiah 44:4 NCV

But I am like an olive tree flourishing in the house of God; I trust in God's unfailing love for ever and ever. Psalm 52:8

Good people will prosper like palm trees. Psalm 92:12 THE MESSAGE

Burst into song, you mountains, you forests and all your trees! Isaiah 44:23

Let the fields be jubilant, and everything in them. Then all the trees of the forest will sing for joy. Psalm 96:12

Praise the Lord . . . you mountains and all hills, fruit trees and all cedars. Psalm 148:7-9

Each tree is recognized by its own fruit. People do not pick figs from thornbushes, or grapes from briers. Luke 6:44

The fruit of the Spirit is love, joy, peace, patience, kindness, goodness, faithfulness, gentleness and self-control. Galatians 5:22-23

For as the soil makes the sprout come up and a garden causes seeds to grow, so the Sovereign LORD will make righteousness and praise spring up before all nations. Isaiah 61:11

Chapter Passages

Matthew 13
Mark 4:31-32
Isaiah 44:3-4

Chapter 6—Our neighbors in the rainforest

Main Verse

"A new command I give you: Love one another. As I have loved you, so you must love one another.
By this all men will know that you are my disciples, if you love one another." John 13:34

Chapter Verses

He who guards his lips guards his life, but he who speaks rashly will come to ruin. Proverbs 13:3

"Don't become so well-adjusted to your culture that you fit into it without even thinking." Romans 12:2 THE MESSAGE

No one can serve two masters. Either he will hate the one and love the other, or he will be devoted to the one and despise the other. You cannot serve both God and Money. Matthew 6:24

Children, obey your parents in the Lord: for this is right. Ephesians 6:1 KJV

The entire law is summed up in a single command: "Love your neighbor as yourself." Galatians 5:14

Chapter Passages

Luke 10:25-37
Matthew 25:31-46

Answer Key

Page 18

Across
1. compost
5. stewardship
9. reduce
10. landfill
11. reuse

Down
1. conservation
2. pesticide
3. habitat
4. hypocrisy
6. dominion
7. herbicide
8. recycle

Page 24

1-4. Answers may vary. See explanations on page 23 (Rainbow Maxims). Bonus: *He replied, "When evening comes, you say, 'It will be fair weather, for the sky is red,' and in the morning, 'Today it will be stormy, for the sky is red and overcast.'*

Page 25

1. barley loaves and fish
2. "Gather the pieces that are left over. Let nothing be wasted."
3. Answers may vary.
4. a net that caught all kinds of fish
5. in a fish's mouth
6. They were fishermen.
7. After fishing unsuccessfully all night, Jesus told them where to fish and they caught so many fish, their nets began to break.

Page 29

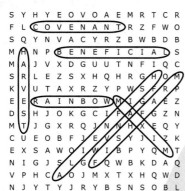

Page 43

1. sustainable farming
2. overgrazing
3. hedgerows or fencerows
4. erosion
5. We can get our food from organic and sustainable farms.
6. *"I will send you rain in its season, and the ground will yield its crops and the trees of the field their fruit."*

Page 47

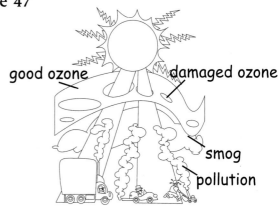

good ozone — damaged ozone — smog — pollution

Page 51

A. 5
B. 1
C. 2
D. 3
E. 6
F. 4

Page 53

1. fossil fuels
2. ground-level ozone, poor
3. smog
4. ozone
5. consider, paying attention, creation

Page 60

1. water, air, sunlight, food
2. its bark
3. its roots
4. trunks should be labeled
5. our arms

Page 62

1. world
2. fruit
3. praise
4. seeds

Page 76

command, neighbor, export, graze, disciple, deforestation, jungle, connotation
"Love your neighbor as yourself."